Bigfoot

by Jacqueline Laks Gorman

Gareth Stevens Publishing
A WORLD ALMANAC EDUCATION GROUP COMPANY

Please visit our web site at: www.garethstevens.com
For a free color catalog describing Gareth Stevens Publishing's
list of high-quality books and multimedia programs,
call 1-800-542-2595 (USA) or 1-800-387-3178 (Canada).
Gareth Stevens Publishing's fax: (414) 332-3567.

Library of Congress Cataloging-in-Publication Data

Gorman, Jacqueline Laks, 1955-
    Bigfoot / by Jacqueline Laks Gorman.
        p. cm. — (X science: an imagination library series)
    Includes bibliographical references and index.
    Summary: An introduction to the large ape-like creature that has reportedly been
seen in parts of the Pacific Northwest.
    ISBN 0-8368-3197-7 (lib. bdg.)
    1. Sasquatch—Juvenile literature. [1. Sasquatch.] I. Title. II. Series.
QL89.2.S2G68   2002
001.944—dc21   2002022531

First published in 2002 by
Gareth Stevens Publishing
A World Almanac Education Group Company
330 West Olive Street, Suite 100
Milwaukee, WI 53212 USA

Text: Jacqueline Laks Gorman
Cover design and page layout: Tammy Gruenewald
Series editor: Betsy Rasmussen
Picture Researcher: Diane Laska-Swanke

Photo credits: Cover, p. 13 Photo Patterson/Gimlin, © 1968 René Dahinden/Fortean
Picture Library; pp. 5, 11, 17 © René Dahinden/Fortean Picture Library; p. 7 © William M.
Rebsamen/Fortean Picture Library; p. 9 © Tony Healy/Fortean Picture Library; p. 15
© Kenneth Garrett/NGS Image Collection; p. 19 © Richard Svensson/Fortean Picture
Library; p. 21 © Fahrenbach/Visuals Unlimited

Printed in the United States of America

1 2 3 4 5 6 7 8 9 06 05 04 03 02

Front cover: This shot is from a 1967
movie. The man who made the movie
says that Bigfoot is a mysterious creature.

TABLE OF CONTENTS

Words that appear in the glossary are printed in **boldface** type the first time they occur in the text.

A BIGFOOT ADVENTURE

A man named Albert Ostman claimed to have had an amazing adventure in 1924. He said that one night while he was camping alone in British Columbia, Canada, a large creature picked him up in his sleeping bag. He said the creature carried him for hours, and it was not until morning that he could see it.

He claimed the creature was a member of a family of giant apelike beasts called Bigfoot — an 8-foot (2.4-meters) father, a 7-foot (2.1-m) mother, a son, and a daughter. Ostman said the family kept him for six days until he was able to run away.

Albert Ostman (*right*) did not tell anyone about his Bigfoot adventure until 1957. He knew many people would not believe him.

WHAT IS BIGFOOT?

Bigfoot is described as a humanlike or apelike creature, covered with black or brown fur. People in many parts of the United States and Canada, especially in the Pacific Northwest, claim to have seen this creature.

Bigfoot is said to be 6 to 9 feet (1.8 to 2.7 m) tall and very strong. It smells bad and has large feet. Bigfoot walks upright and eats roots, berries, deer, and elk. It is supposed to be very shy and afraid of people, but curious about them, too.

Bigfoot is also known by other names, such as *Skookum* and *Sasquatch*, a Native American name meaning "wild man."

This painting shows what Bigfoot is supposed to look like. It is based on the many **legends** and stories about the creature.

EARLY SIGHTINGS OF BIGFOOT

For many years, Native American tribes told stories about Bigfoot. Early explorers knew about Bigfoot, as well. The first written report about a Bigfoot came from an explorer named David Thompson, who wrote about large footprints he found in Alberta, Canada, in 1811.

In 1924, a group of miners in Washington reported that they saw some hairy, apelike creatures. They shot at two of them. That night, the miners were trapped in their cabin by a group of creatures that threw rocks and pounded on the doors, walls, and roof.

Many scientists say stories about Bigfoot are legends or lies, but many people say they saw something real.

A Bigfoot researcher named Tony Healy stands next to an 8-foot (2.4-m) statue of Bigfoot. The statue was carved from a redwood tree in Willow Creek, California.

THE FOOTPRINTS OF BIGFOOT

People who believe in Bigfoot say that footprints are the best evidence to prove that the creature exists. In 1958, a man named Jerry Crew found lots of very large footprints near his **bulldozer** in Willow Creek, California. Examining the prints, it seemed as if the creature had been looking at the bulldozer. Crew made **casts** of the prints.

Many other footprints have been found over the years in Washington, Oregon, and western Canada. Some of the most interesting were found in Walla Walla, Washington in 1982. These footprints showed **dermal ridges**. Only humans and **primates** have dermal ridges, which are found on fingers and the soles of feet.

A plaster cast taken of a Bigfoot footprint is much larger than a human's foot. This cast is of a footprint found in Bluff Creek, California, in 1967.

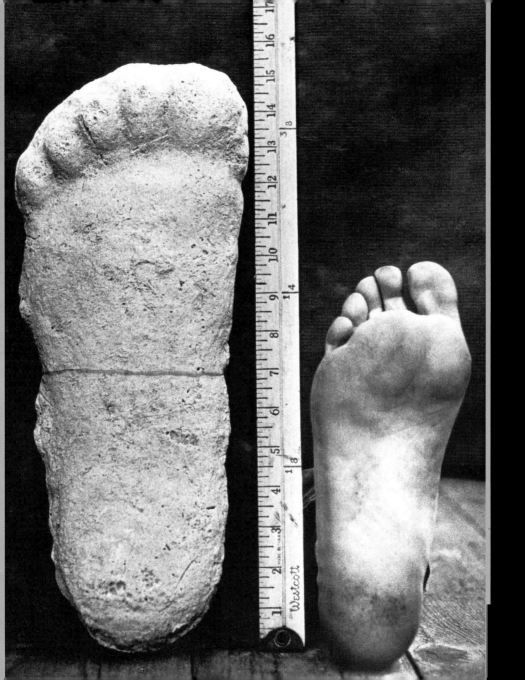

LIVE ON FILM?

In October 1967, a Bigfoot researcher named Roger Patterson and his friend were horseback riding in Bluff Creek, California. They claimed to have seen a creature sitting beside the creek. Patterson said he grabbed his movie camera and filmed the creature as it walked away into the trees.

Patterson's short movie is the only film ever made of Bigfoot. The film seems to show a female, over 6 feet (1.8 m) tall, with a short neck, sloping forehead, long arms, and powerful legs.

Many people think the film is fake. They say it shows a person dressed in a furry suit.

This picture, taken from Patterson's film, shows the creature looking back as it walks away. Bigfoot is supposed to be very curious about people.

WHAT COULD IT BE?

What kind of creature might Bigfoot be? Perhaps it is an animal thought to be extinct that has really survived. The coelacanth, for example, is a fish that was thought to be extinct for 60 million years but was found living in South Africa in 1938. Maybe Bigfoot is an **ancestor** of an early human called a **Neanderthal**. Or maybe it is a type of giant ape known as Gigantopithecus that scientists believe became **extinct** 400,000 years ago.

Perhaps Bigfoot is an animal that no one has yet been able to prove exists. It is possible. No one knew about the giant panda, for example, until it was first seen in 1937. The **Komodo dragon** was seen for the first time in 1956.

Could Bigfoot be an ancestor of a Neanderthal that went to live in wild unexplored places? Here, the skull of a Neanderthal is shown with a computerized image created from it.

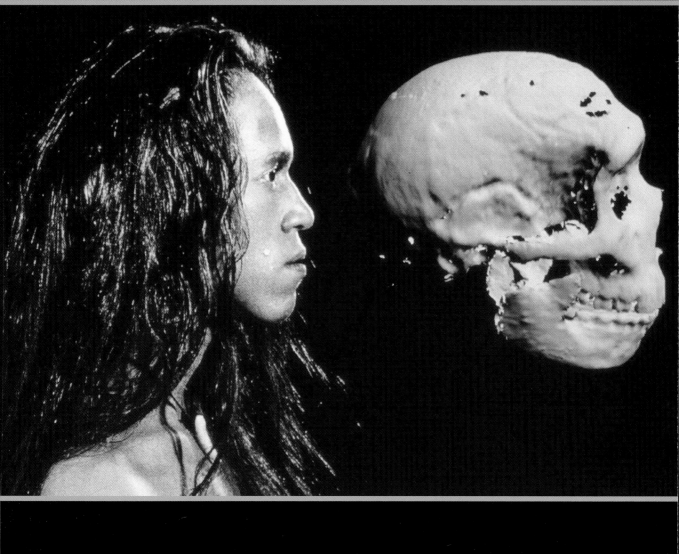

SOME SCIENTISTS WANT MORE PROOF

Most scientists do not believe Bigfoot exists, even though many people say they have seen it, and many footprints have been found. Scientists want real proof. They want someone to trap a live Bigfoot, or they want someone to find the body, skeleton, or skull of a dead Bigfoot.

Bigfoot believers go on **expeditions** to look for proof. Some of them put out food as bait for Bigfoot. Some have made tape recordings of what they say is the voice of Bigfoot. Grunts, howls, and roars can be heard on the tapes. Scientists, however, say the recordings are not real proof.

Dr. Grover Krantz was an **anthropology** professor at Washington State University. He looked for proof that Bigfoot exists. Dr. Krantz said there may be 2,000 Bigfoot in the Pacific Northwest.

BIGFOOT RELATIVES

Other humanlike beasts are said to live in other parts of the world, as well. The most famous beast is the Yeti, which is also called the Abominable Snowman. According to stories, the Yeti lives in the **Himalayas** in Tibet and Nepal. Many mountain climbers have reported finding Yeti tracks in the snow.

Other stories about tall, hairy creatures include the Chinese Wildman in China, Alma in Mongolia, and Yowie in Australia. Could they all be relatives of Bigfoot?

Yeti supposedly lives in the Himalayan Mountains. Deep footprints made by bare feet in the snow have been found on Mount Everest, the tallest mountain in the world.

RECENT DISCOVERIES

Today, people still report seeing Bigfoot or finding the creature's footprints. In September 2000, Bigfoot researchers had exciting news. They found a print they think was made by a Bigfoot's body. From the print, it looks like the creature was lying in the mud and reaching to get some fruit. A plaster cast was made of the body print, and it is called the "Skookum Cast."

The cast appears to show a large, hairy forearm, hip, thigh, and heel. Hairs were taken from the mud stuck to the cast. Some of the hairs appear to come from a primate that has never been identified.

Dr. Jeffrey Meldrum, a professor at Idaho State University, and Dr. Grover Krantz inspect the "Skookum Cast." The cast was made from a print found in Skookum Meadows in Washington.

MORE TO READ AND VIEW

Books (Nonfiction)   *Giant Humanlike Beasts. Unsolved Mysteries* (series). Brian Innes (Raintree Steck-Vaughn)

Sasquatch: Wild Man of North America. Mysteries of Science (series). Elaine Landau (Millbrook Press)

Scary Science: The Truth Behind Vampires, Witches, UFOs, Ghosts and More! Sylvia Funston (Owl Books)

Yeti: Abominable Snowman of the Himalayas. Mysteries of Science (series). Elaine Landau (Millbrook Press)

Books (Fiction)   *Bigfoot Doesn't Square Dance. Adventures of the Bailey School Kids* (series). Debbie Dadey and Marcia Thornton Jones (Little Apple)

The Boy Who Cried Bigfoot. The Zack Files (series). Dan Greenburg (Grosset & Dunlap)

Legend of the Desert Bigfoot. Last Chance Detectives (series). Jake Thoene and Luke Thoene (Tyndale House)

Quest for Bigfoot: A Novel Adventure for Young People. Krya Petrovskaya Wayne (Hancock House)

Sasquatch. Roland Smith (Hyperion)

Snow Monster Mystery. Bailey City Monsters (series). Marcia Thornton Jones and Debbie Dadey (Scholastic)

Videos (Nonfiction)   *Ancient Mysteries: Bigfoot.* (A&E)

Videos (Fiction)   *Bigfoot: The Unforgettable Encounter.* (Republic Studios)
Harry and the Hendersons. (Universal Studios)

WEB SITES

Web sites change frequently, but we believe the following web sites are going to last. You can also use good search engines, such as **Yahooligans!** [**www.yahooligans.com**] or **Google** [**www.google.com**] to find more information about Bigfoot. Some keywords that will help you are: *Bigfoot, Sasquatch, Yeti,* and *Abominable Snowman.*

www.ajkids.com

Ask Jeeves Kids, the junior Ask Jeeves site, is a great place to do research. Try asking:

What is Sasquatch?

What is the Abominable Snowman?

You can also just type in words and phrases with "?" at the end, such as:

Bigfoot?

Yeti?

www.yahooligans.com

This junior version of the Yahoo site is very easy to use. Simply type in the word "Bigfoot" to get a list of sites that are appropriate for kids.

www.unmuseum.org

The *Museum of Unnatural Mystery* is an online museum of strange things. The "Lost Worlds Exhibition" allows you to read about cryptozoology, the study of creatures that are not proven to exist.

www.cryptozoology.com

Devoted to the study of unseen animals, the *Cryptozoology* site has information on Bigfoot and other interesting beasts.

www.bfro.net

This site of the *Bigfoot Field Researchers Organization,* which describes itself as the "only scientific organization probing the Bigfoot/Sasquatch mystery," has information on the Bigfoot legend, sightings and encounters, and the latest research.

www.ratsnest.net/bigfoot

In addition to many stories and reports of encounters, this *Bigfoot* site has art and lots of links to related topics.

www.cgocable.net/~rgavel/links/bigfoot.html

Maintained by a believer, this *Bigfoot* site contains many reports of encounters and the text of a story written by Teddy Roosevelt in 1892 about a Bigfoot attack.

GLOSSARY

You can find these words on the pages listed. Reading a word in a sentence helps you understand it even better.

ancestor (ANN-sehs-tohr) — a person in a family who came before or earlier. 14

anthropology (an-thruh-PAHLL-uh-jee) — the study of people. 16

bulldozer (BUL-dohz-urr) — a tractor with a big flat shovel on the front used for moving earth. 10

casts (KASTS) — impressions that are formed when soft material is poured into molds. 10, 20

dermal ridges (DER-muhl RIJ-izz) — lines like fingerprints that are found on the hands and feet of humans and apes. 10

expeditions (eks-puh-DIHSH-uhns) — trips taken for a special purpose. 16

extinct (eks-TEENKT) — with no more members of a species left alive. 14

Himalayas (him-uh-LAY-uhs) — mountains in southern Asia. 18

Komodo dragon (kuh-MOH-doh DRAYG-uhn) — the largest of all known lizards. 14

legends (LEHJ-ehnds) — stories coming down from the past. 6, 8

Neanderthal (nee-ANN-dur-thall) — an extinct subspecies of humans, like a caveman. 14

primates (PRY-mayts) — members of a group of intelligent mammals including humans, apes, and monkeys. 10, 20

INDEX